# CONTENTS

# CHAPTER 1

# HOT or COLD but ALWAYS DRY

Picture a desert. Do you imagine something hot, dry and empty? It's true that deserts are dry, but only some are hot. And deserts can be full of life.

Deserts are a type of habitat. The other main habitats are forests, grasslands, tundra and **aquatic**. Each type of habitat has a particular **climate**. Each has animals and plants that can live there. Plants, animals and people have all **adapted** to desert living. Some of these adaptations are wild!

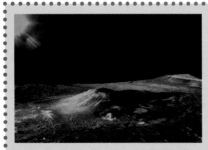

**FACT BOX**
Earth isn't the only planet with deserts. Mars is cold and extremely dry. The entire planet is one big desert!

EXPLORING EARTH'S HABITATS

# DESERT HABITATS
## AROUND THE WORLD

M. M. Eboch

Raintree is an imprint of Capstone Global Library Limited, a company incorporated in England and Wales having its registered office at 264 Banbury Road, Oxford, OX2 7DY – Registered company number: 6695582

www.raintree.co.uk
myorders@raintree.co.uk

Edited by Gina Kammer
Designed by Julie Peters
Original illustrations © Capstone Global Library Limited 2020
Picture research by Morgan Walters
Production by Kathy McColley
Originated by Capstone Global Library Ltd
Printed and bound in India

ISBN: 978 1 4747 8572 3 (hardback)
ISBN: 978 1 4747 8585 3 (paperback)

**British Library Cataloguing in Publication Data**
A full catalogue record for this book is available from the British Library.

**Acknowledgements**
We would like to thank the following for permission to reproduce photographs: Alamy: Robert Fried, bottom right 8; Getty Images: FADEL SENNA, bottom 25; National Geographic: John Kappler, 29; Newscom: Anthony Bannister/NHPA/Photoshot, top right 15, OMAR KAMAL, VINCENT LEFAI AFP, middle 25; Shutterstock: Andrei Rybachuk, 12, Anton Foltin, bottom 10, Aresium Images, spread 24-25, spread 26-27, spread 28-29, Arlene Waller, spread 14-15, spread 16-17, spread 18-19, spread 20-21, spread 22-23, Bildagentur Zoonar GmbH, bottom left 15, Charles T. Peden, 16, 18, Danita Delmont, top 13, Elena11, bottom 4, Ernst Prettenthaler, bottom 6, Iryna Rasko, 20, Jonathan L Torres, background design element , Kekyalyaynen, 23, Ken Wolter, 9, kojihirano, 17, lady-luck, (vector plants) Cover, loskutnikov, (sun) Cover, LutsenkoLarissa, bottom 27, nashiihsan, 21, Oleg Gekman, (girl) Cover, Photonell_DD2017, 14, Sergey Novikov, spread 4-5, spread 6-7, tntphototravis, top 11, Tom Roche, spread 8-9, spread 10-11, spread 12-13, Tomasz Mazon, top 27, ventdusud, (valley) Cover, Wojciech Dziadosz, bottom 7, Yusiki, top 5

Every effort has been made to contact copyright holders of material reproduced in this book. Any omissions will be rectified in subsequent printings if notice is given to the publisher.

All the internet addresses (URLs) given in this book were valid at the time of going to press. However, due to the dynamic nature of the internet, some addresses may have changed, or sites may have changed or ceased to exist since publication. While the author and publisher regret any inconvenience this may cause readers, no responsibility for any such changes can be accepted by either the author or the publisher.

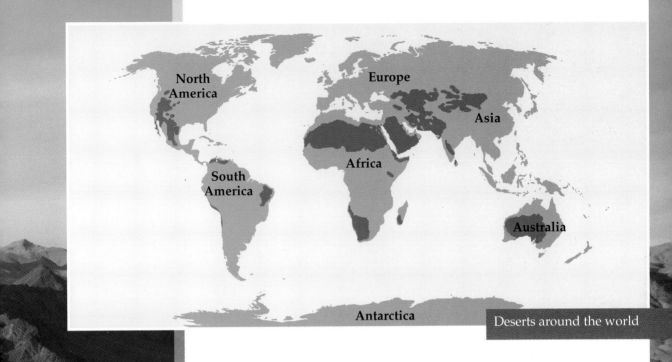

North America

Europe

Asia

Africa

South America

Australia

Antarctica

Deserts around the world

## WHAT MAKES A DESERT?

Deserts are found around the world. All these deserts share certain features. The most important is **precipitation**. A desert receives less than 25 centimetres of moisture a year. In the UK, the average rainfall is about three times that.

The driest desert in the world is the Atacama Desert in Chile, South America. It only gets measurable rain every 5 to 20 years!

**adapt**  change in order to survive; a change in an animal or plant to better fit its environment is called an adaptation
**aquatic**   to do with water
**climate**  usual weather conditions in a place
**precipitation**  moisture that lands on the ground, including rain, snow, hail, mist or fog

Little rain means few clouds and lots of sun. All that sun means many deserts are hot. Does the desert you pictured have sand dunes and camels? You may be thinking of the Sahara in Africa. About 2.5 million people live there, mainly in areas close to sources of water. Sahara temperatures can rise to more than 50 degrees Celsius.

The United States has deserts. Death Valley in California is the hottest place on Earth. Only a few hundred people live there. In one area, the average daily high in July and August is 46°C. Death Valley gets less than 7.6 cm of rain a year.

**FACT BOX**
The world's highest recorded temperature was in Death Valley: 56.7°C.

Death Valley in California, USA

Antarctica is the coldest place on the planet. Huge windstorms pick up snow from the ground and turn into blizzards. Yet Antarctica gets very little precipitation. That makes it a desert – the largest one on Earth. The world's second-largest desert, the Arctic Desert, is also cold. This desert gets between 15 and 25 cm of precipitation every year. Most of that falls as snow. Antarctica has no native populations, but the Arctic is home to 4 million people.

Deserts cover about one-fifth of Earth's surface. It's easier to live where water is plentiful. Despite this, deserts support a variety of life, including people.

Desert in Antarctica

# CHAPTER 2

# LIVING THE DRY LIFE: PLANTS IN THE DESERT

Just as people need water to survive, so do plants. Desert plants have unique ways of getting water. They can also store water for long periods.

The cactus is perhaps the best-known desert plant. Cacti have spines instead of leaves. The spines don't lose moisture like leaves do. Spines may be long, stiff and sharp, like large needles. Or they may look almost soft, like short, white hair. Some have hooked barbs on the ends. Spines make it harder for animals to eat the plants. It doesn't stop everyone, though. Prickly pears have flat pads covered in spines. Some people eat the pads like a vegetable. Countries such as Mexico, Italy and South Africa grow cactus as a crop.

A man eats the pad of a prickly pear cactus.

Cactus flesh stores water. Mule deer, bighorn sheep and hares know they can find water inside. Humans have learned this trick too. A hiker who gets lost in the desert might find water by cutting open a cactus. However, only certain types of cacti, such as a barrel cactus, contain drinkable water.

Barrel cacti

### FACT BOX

Some deserts have few plants of any kind. In polar deserts, most of the land is always covered in ice. The ice-free coasts hold almost all life in these areas.

About 2,000 different kinds of cacti exist around the world. They can look like barrels, blades of grass, pin-cushions or even starfish. Firm, waxy skin holds in the water. Some cacti have very long but shallow roots. Saguaro cactus roots are usually about 10 to 15 cm deep. Yet they can extend to 15 metres to soak up the water from a light rain.

Organ pipe cacti

A woodpecker and bee feed on the blooms of a Saguaro cactus.

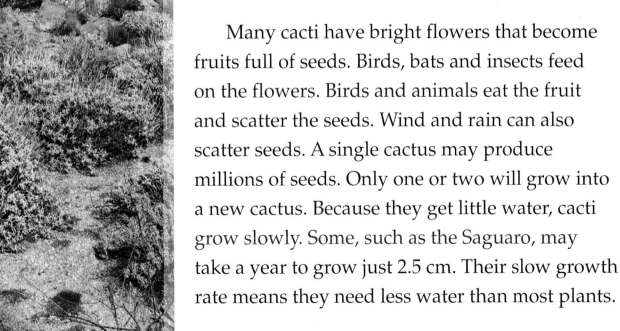

Many cacti have bright flowers that become fruits full of seeds. Birds, bats and insects feed on the flowers. Birds and animals eat the fruit and scatter the seeds. Wind and rain can also scatter seeds. A single cactus may produce millions of seeds. Only one or two will grow into a new cactus. Because they get little water, cacti grow slowly. Some, such as the Saguaro, may take a year to grow just 2.5 cm. Their slow growth rate means they need less water than most plants.

Aloe plants also have thick leaves that store water. The leaves are filled with a jelly-like material. This gel stores water and energy for the plant. People use the gel to soothe burns, including sunburn. As the gel is mainly water, it adds moisture to burnt skin. The substance that gives the plants energy helps heal human skin. For these uses, aloe plants are grown in dry areas around the world as crops.

Aloe plants

Century plant

Century plants have a base of thick, sword-like leaves. From the middle, a tall, thin flower stalk rises up to 9 metres high. Native Americans found many uses for the century plant. People can eat the base, stalk, seeds and sap. The tough fibres can be woven into rope or rough cloth. Thorns on the leaves make good pins and needles.

**FACT BOX**

Century plants' leaves and roots foam when they are chopped and cooked. People have used this foam as soap.

# CHAPTER 3

# KEEPING COOL:
# ANIMAL
# ADAPTATIONS

If plants can survive in the desert, so can animals. They just need ways to handle the temperature, sun and lack of water. Camels can go for weeks without eating or drinking. They have two rows of eyelashes to keep dust out of their eyes. They can even close their nostrils so they won't snort sand! These adaptations make camels perfect for carrying passengers with goods to trade across deserts.

Armadillo lizards live in the deserts of southern Africa. They hide in the cracks and crevices of large rocks. Their skin colours blend in with the rocks, hiding them from **predators**. They eat desert plants and animals, such as scorpions. Meanwhile, birds of prey try to eat them. The frightened lizard puts its tail in its mouth and rolls into a ball. Then it's protected by its tough skin. The armadillo lizard can also drop its tail to escape.

An armadillo lizard curls up for protection.

Thorny devil

In Australia, the thorny devil lizard has spikes all over its body. This protects it from predators. It gets moisture when dew settles onto its skin. Grooves between its spikes draw the water towards the lizard's mouth.

**predator** animal that hunts other animals for food

Some desert animals come out only at night when it's cooler. Other animals are active only at dawn and at dusk. These are the times to watch out for rattlesnakes! A few animals slow down when it's too hot or dry. The round-tailed ground squirrel sleeps through the summer. Desert toads sleep deep underground. They come out only when summer rains fill desert ponds.

Ground squirrel

Some birds live in the desert only during certain seasons. They can fly long distances to find food or water. The tall Saguaro cacti offer a great view. Hawks perch on top to search for food over long distances. They may build nests of sticks between the cactus arms. Woodpeckers dig out nest cavities inside the cactus. If they stop using a nest, sparrows and other birds may move in.

A Harris's hawk perches on a Saguaro cactus.

Cacti provide the animals with food as well. Bats and insects get **nectar** and **pollen** from flowers. Many small animals eat the ripe fruit.

A ground squirrel eats the fruit of a prickly pear cactus.

Cacti even provide homes to animals such as the wood rat, also called the pack rat. These rats may build a den at the base of the cactus or use pieces of cacti in their dens. The cacti spines help protect the rats from predators such as foxes and coyotes.

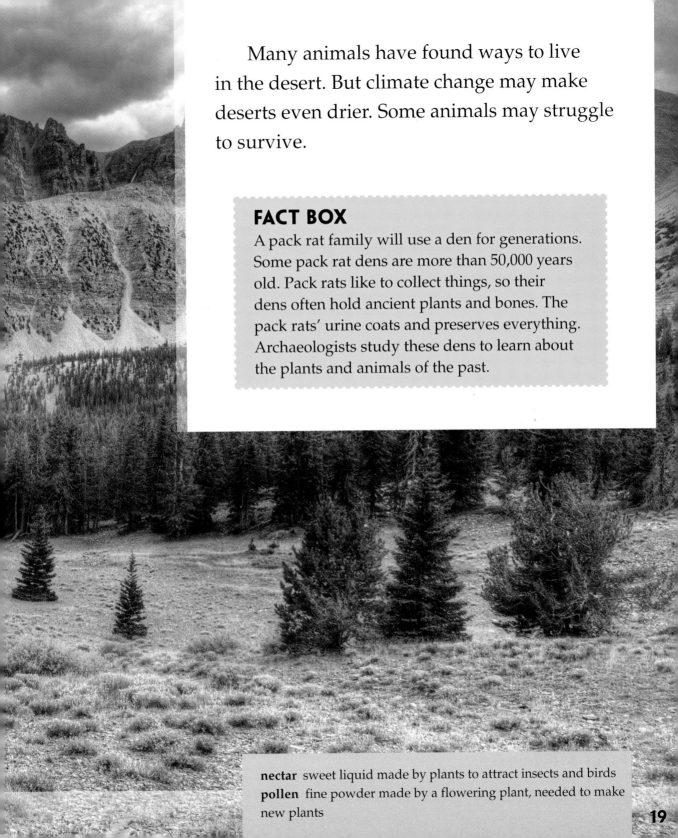

Many animals have found ways to live in the desert. But climate change may make deserts even drier. Some animals may struggle to survive.

**FACT BOX**

A pack rat family will use a den for generations. Some pack rat dens are more than 50,000 years old. Pack rats like to collect things, so their dens often hold ancient plants and bones. The pack rats' urine coats and preserves everything. Archaeologists study these dens to learn about the plants and animals of the past.

**nectar** sweet liquid made by plants to attract insects and birds
**pollen** fine powder made by a flowering plant, needed to make new plants

# CHAPTER 4

# AT HOME IN THE HEAT: HUMANS IN DESERTS

People need water to survive. Deserts have few rivers, streams or lakes. Yet people have lived in deserts for thousands of years. Many were **nomads**. They travelled to different places to find water and food with each season. They often hunted and harvested wild plants. Some raised animals adapted to desert living, such as camels.

Today over 1 billion people live in deserts. That's one-seventh of the world's population! But how do they manage the dry, hot climate?

People lead camels through the desert.

A camp in the Sahara Desert

People may dig wells to find water deep underground. They may also use **irrigation** to move water from wetter regions. In large deserts, people gather near oases. An oasis is a fertile piece of land around a fresh water supply. A few have enough water to support a village or a city. In the Sahara, two-thirds of the people live in oases. They use the water to grow fruit trees, vegetables and grains.

Today trucks bring food grown in other places to people in the desert. Air-conditioning keeps buildings cool. Modern irrigation methods can bring water from further away.

**irrigation** act of supplying water to land in order to grow plants
**nomad** person who moves from place to place to find food and water, rather than living in one spot

In America, millions of people have moved to the Southwest. People like the region's warm temperatures and lack of rain. These benefits are also challenges. Desert cities must find ways to supply enough water. Some do water recycling to reuse **wastewater**. Wastewater can be used for irrigation or in factories. For these uses, the water doesn't have to be safe to drink. It takes more work to make water safe for drinking.

Population change in the United States from 1 July 2017 to 1 July 2018

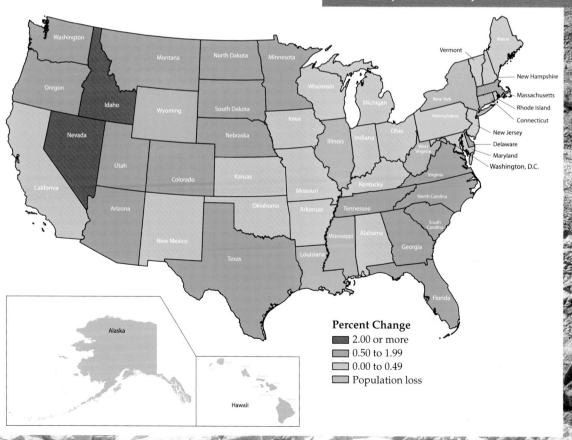

**Percent Change**
- 2.00 or more
- 0.50 to 1.99
- 0.00 to 0.49
- Population loss

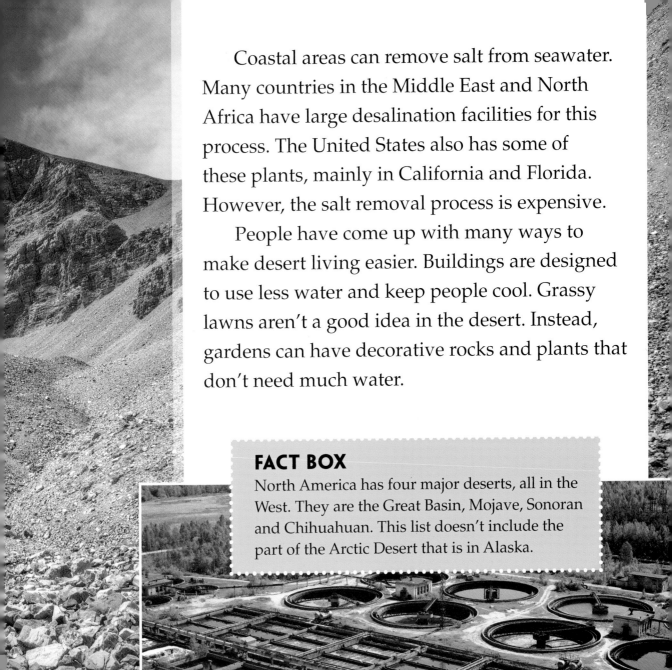

Coastal areas can remove salt from seawater. Many countries in the Middle East and North Africa have large desalination facilities for this process. The United States also has some of these plants, mainly in California and Florida. However, the salt removal process is expensive.

People have come up with many ways to make desert living easier. Buildings are designed to use less water and keep people cool. Grassy lawns aren't a good idea in the desert. Instead, gardens can have decorative rocks and plants that don't need much water.

**FACT BOX**

North America has four major deserts, all in the West. They are the Great Basin, Mojave, Sonoran and Chihuahuan. This list doesn't include the part of the Arctic Desert that is in Alaska.

A water recycling sewage treatment station

**wastewater** water that has been used by people

# CHAPTER 5

# DESERTS GROWING AND DYING

Deserts have a major **natural resource** – lots of sun. The sunlight makes deserts ideal areas for **solar power**. Morocco has built a huge solar power plant in the Sahara. It looks like an ocean of reflective mirrors. Workers have to wear sunglasses to protect their eyes from the blinding glare. Thousands of mirrors direct the sun's rays to a tube. The sun heats a liquid in the tube. It produces steam, which powers an engine to make electricity. The site can provide electricity to more than 1 million people.

Deserts have other resources as well. Many are home to valuable metals such as gold, silver and iron. Some deserts have large oil and natural gas deposits. These can be turned into electricity or fuel for vehicles.

In the USA, Utah's Great Salt Lake Desert is a major source of sodium chloride. Sodium chloride is commonly known as salt. The Great Salt Lake is very salty. Its water is left in shallow pools to **evaporate**. The salt left behind is collected for cooking and other uses.

SPAIN

ATLANTIC
OCEAN

Noor 1

RABAT   Fes
Casablanca

MOROCCO

Airport

Marrakech

Ouarzazate
Ouarzazate

Agadir

ALGERIA

Zag

200 km          4 km

WESTERN SAHARA

Noor solar power plant in Morocco

**evaporate**  change from liquid into gas
**natural resource**  material found in nature that people use, such as soil, air, trees, coal and oil
**solar power**  energy from the sun that can be used for heating and electricity

Humans living in deserts have brought changes, including introducing invasive species. Native species are plants and animals that have lived in a place for centuries. They've adapted naturally over time. Invasive species are plants or animals that arrived recently. They may not have natural enemies. They can grow out of control and take over. If native species can't compete, they die out. This process can change and harm deserts and other habitats.

Sometimes invasive plants arrive by accident. Seeds are carried on shoes, by birds or in the wind. People also introduce invasive species on purpose. The southwestern United States has changed hugely in the last two centuries. People brought livestock such as cows, which ate the desert grasses. This made room for invasive plants. People also planted invasive salt cedar trees because they liked how they look. Salt cedar thrives in the desert's high heat and poor soil. The tree's deep roots drink any available water. They then release salt crystals that poison the ground and kill other plants.

Salt cedar

Deserts are valuable, but that doesn't mean we want more of them. Yet some areas are turning into deserts. This process is called **desertification**. It may happen during a long **drought**. Cutting down trees can cause desertification. So can poor farming practices or using too much water for people and farms. Today climate change is turning more areas into deserts. Rivers dry up. Patterns of rain and snow change. Many plants die, and animals can't find food.

**FACT BOX**

As the planet warms, precipitation will increase. Scientists expect the Arctic to get less snow and much more rain. This change will affect Arctic animals such as reindeer and polar bears.

People in Africa are trying to stop desertification around the Sahara. They are planting a 14-km-wide strand of plants that can resist drought. They hope to create a barrier to stop the desert spreading. This "Great Green Wall" is 15 per cent complete.

### THE GREAT GREEN WALL INITIATIVE

MAURITANIA · MALI · NIGER · CHAD · SUDAN · ERITREA · DJIBOUTI · SENEGAL · BURKINA FASO · NIGERIA · ETHIOPIA

PARTICIPATING COUNTRIES

FOCUS AREA

The Great Green Wall's goal is to stretch about 8,000 km from Djibouti to Senegal.

When the desert is damaged, it doesn't heal easily. Deserts must be managed well. Keeping cars on roads and trails is one way. It may mean keeping people out of some areas completely. With care, we can all keep enjoying deserts. They are important both to us and our planet.

### FACT BOX

What can you do? Many cities use too much water. The water supply will eventually run out. People can help by using less water. Instead of planting a lawn, use decorative rocks and low-water native plants. This is a good practice everywhere, especially in the desert. You can search "conserve water" online for more ideas.

**desertification** process by which land becomes desert
**drought** long period of weather with little or no rain

# GLOSSARY

**adapt** change in order to survive; a change in an animal or plant to better fit its environment is called an adaptation

**aquatic** to do with water

**climate** usual weather conditions in a place

**desertification** process by which land becomes desert

**drought** long period of weather with little or no rain

**evaporate** change from liquid into gas

**irrigation** act of supplying water to land in order to grow plants

**natural resource** material found in nature that people use, such as soil, air, trees, coal and oil

**nectar** sweet liquid made by plants to attract insects and birds

**nomad** person who moves from place to place to find food and water, rather than living in one spot

**pollen** fine powder made by a flowering plant, needed to make new plants

**precipitation** moisture that lands on the ground, including rain, snow, hail, mist or fog

**predator** animal that hunts other animals for food

**solar power** energy from the sun that can be used for heating and electricity

**wastewater** water that has been used by people

# FIND OUT MORE

## BOOKS

*Amazing Deserts Around the World* (Passport to Nature), Rachel Castro (Raintree, 2019)

*Habitats and Biomes* (Earth by Numbers), Nancy Dickmann (Raintree, 2018)

*Protecting Our Planet* (Beyond the Headlines!), Jilly Hunt (Raintree, 2018)

## WEBSITES

**bbc.co.uk/bitesize/topics/zx882hv/articles/zsqnfg8**
Watch this short film to learn more about the desert habitat, including how some plants and animals have adapted to live there.

**dkfindout.com/uk/search/deserts**
Find out more about different types of deserts, including their weather systems, habitats and ecosystems.

# COMPREHENSION QUESTIONS

1. Many desert animals are at risk. Should anything be done to protect them? How do you think people could help?

2. People use technology to make desert life easier. What is good about desert technology? What might be bad? Do you think technology will help in the future? Or will it do more harm than good?

3. Every year, many people move to deserts. They then need water for many uses. Should cities have to provide all the water people want? Should people have to use less water than they want? How should water use be managed?

# INDEX